Contents

Learn HTML in Two Hours

1.1 Introduction to HTML

- HyperText Markup Language (HTML) is a language used for creating web pages.
- It is a web authoring software language specifically created for making World Wide Web pages.
- The language contains mark up tags that direct how the page is to be displayed in a browser.
- It can be created using a simple text editor.
- The created file is stored with the extension .html or .htm.
- The executable file can be viewed in a web browser, like, Google Chrome and Internet Explorer.

1.2 Create HTML document

Perform the following steps to create a blank HTML file.

1. **Open Text editor.**
   - If the operating system of your computer is Windows, you can use *Notepad*.
   - If you have Apple computer, you can use *TextEdit*.
   - If you have Linux Ubuntu operating system, you can use *gedit*.

Code in Notepad

2. **Write HTML program.**

We shall see how to write the program subsequently. For now, simply write-

- `<html>` - this indicates starting of the HTML document
- `</html>` - this indicates ending of the HTML document.

Code in Notepad

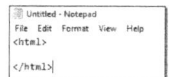

3. **Save the file.**

- Click `<File>` `<Save As>`.
- Select the folder where you want to save the file.
- Type a filename. For example, `myprog.html`
- Select the file extension as `.htm` or `.html`.
- Click `<Save>`.

4. **Run the HTML file.**

- In the directory, Right click on the file with .html extension.
- Click `<Open with>`.
- Select the browser in which you want to view the web page. For example, Google Chrome, Internet Explorer, Firefox Mozilla.
- The web page opens in the browser. You can see the filename on the top.

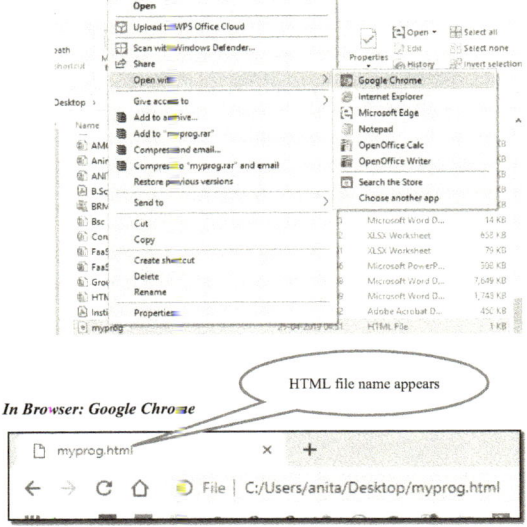

In Browser: Google Chrome

HTML file name appears

5. **View source code of the displayed web page.**

- Right click on the web page.
- Click <View Page Source>. The source code is displayed.

4

In Browser: Google Chrome

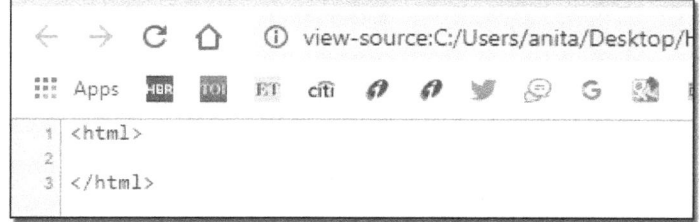

1.3 Tag in HTML

- HTML consists of tags.
- HTML tags are used for formatting of text.
- Tags are instructions for the browser to be applied on the enclosing text.
- Without tags, the text in browser will appear as simple text, without any formatting.
- For example, tags are used to display text in color, bold, italics and many more.
- To identify a tag, they are placed within angular brackets <>.
- Mostly, the tags are used in pairs –
    - start tag within angular braces, and
    - end tag starting with backslash followed by same tag.
    - For example, <u> and </u>.
- The tag applies on the content in between the start and end tag. For example,
    - <u> implies start of the tag underline.
    - Next the content on which the tag is to be applied is placed.
    - Then, end of the tag </u> is written.
    - In the following example, we see that the content within the start tag <u> and end tag </u> is only underlined.

```
This statement shows use of <u> underline </u> tag
```

In Browser, it is displayed as-

This statement shows use of underline tag

1.4 Components of HTML document

- **DOCTYPE** or Document type is used for indicating the version of HTML used in a web page. Using this, the web page appears similar in the different web browsers.
- A HTML document consists of headings, sub-headings, tables, etc., which provide a structure to the document.
- **<html> </html>.** All HTML documents start and end with this tag.
- HTML document is mainly divided into two parts - Head and Body.
- **Head** is the header section of a document. It contains tags that are to be executed before the content in body element is displayed to the user.
  - **<head> </head>.** It contains information about a web page.
  - **<Title> </Title>.** The content written within title tag is displayed as the title of a web page. Title is used by search engine to create index of content.
- A simple basic structure of HTML document is as follows –

```
<!DOCTYPE html>
<html>
<head>
<title>My First HTML Program</title>
</head>
</html>
```

In Browser, it is displayed as-

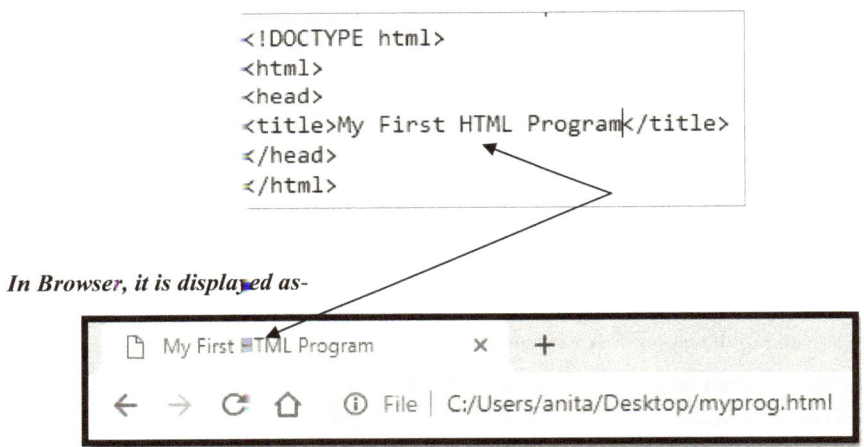

- **Body** contains body content and is displayed in the web browser.
  - **<body> </body>** tags enclose most HTML elements used within the body.
  - **<!--> <-->** are comment tags. The comment is not visible on the browser. It is useful to write comments in source code.

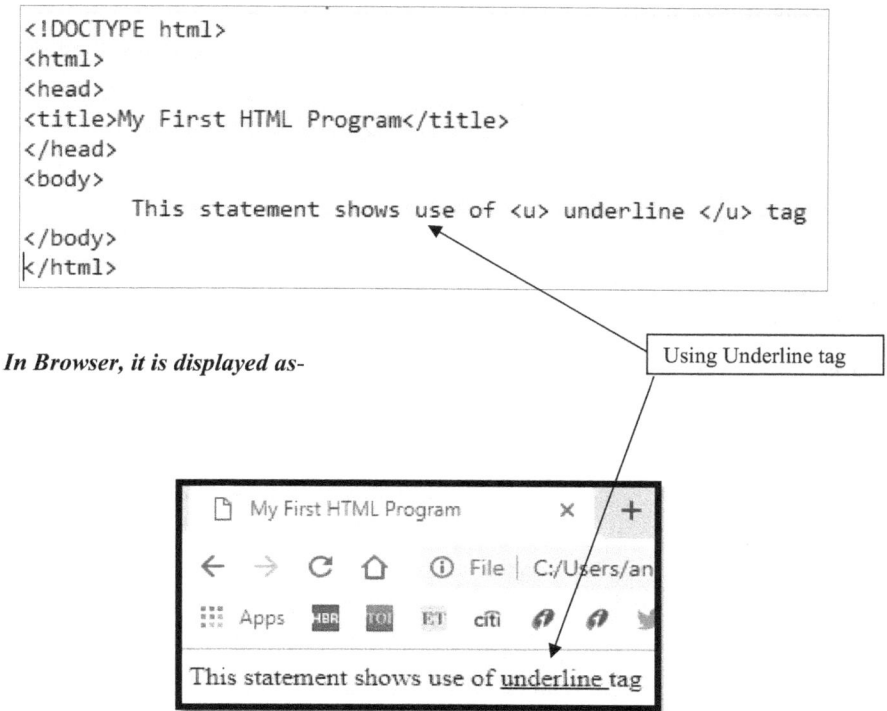

1.5 HTML Commands

Here, the common commands in HTML are described briefly.

1.5.1 Text formatting

The text content of a web page can be formatted to make it more attractive by using different tags. The tags for text formatting discussed here are - Heading, Emphasize, Italics, Strong, Bold, Underline, Mark, Big, Small, Subscript, Superscript, Pre text, insert, delete, break and horizontal line. The tags are summarized in Table 1.

Table 1. Some Tags in HTML

S. No	Tag Name	Tag	Tag Description
1	Heading	\<h1> \</h1> … \<h6> \</h6>	Six levels of heading elements from H1 to H6. H1 has the largest text size and H6 has the smallest text size.
2	Emphasize	\<em> \</em>	To make a text more pronounced in a sentence. Emphasized text is displayed in italics.
3	Italics	\<i> \</i>	Enclosed text is displayed in typographic italics.
4	Strong	\<strong> \</strong>	Enclosed text is displayed in bold.
5	Bold	\<b> \</b>	Enclosed text is displayed in bold.
6	Underline	\<u> \</u>	Enclosed text is underlined.
7	Mark	\<mark> \</mark>	Enclosed text is highlighted.
8	Big	\<big> \</big>	Enclosed text is bigger in size than the rest of the text.
9	Small	\<small> \</small>	Enclosed text is smaller in size than rest of the text.
10	Subscript	_\	Enclosed text is displayed as subscript
11	Superscript	\[\]	Enclosed text is displayed as superscript.
12	Pre Text	\<pre> \</pre>	Enclosed text is displayed as it is - in terms of position, font size, font type etc.
13	Delete-Insert	\<del> and \</del> \<ins> and \</ins>	Enclosed text is displayed as struck out. Enclosed text is underlined
14	Break	\ 	No closing tag is needed. Used for line spacing. For multiple line spacing, use the tag repeatedly.
15	Horizontal line	\<hr>	No closing tag is needed. To insert a horizontal line in the web page.

Code

```html
<!DOCTYPE html>
<html>
<head>
<title>Text Formatting</title>
</head>
<body>
<h1>h1 - This is a beautiful world. </h1>
<h2>h2 - This is a beautiful world. </h2>
<h3>h3 - This is a beautiful world. </h3>
<h4>h4 - This is a beautiful world. </h4>
<h5>h5 - This is a beautiful world. </h5>
<h6>h6 - This is a beautiful world. </h6>
<hr>
<p> 2. Emphasis (em) - This is a <em>beautiful </em> world. </p>
<p> 3. Italics (i) - This is a <i>beautiful </i> world.</p>
<p> 4. Strong (strong) This is a <strong>beautiful </strong> world.</p>
<p> 5. Bold (bold) This is a <bold> beautiful </bold> world. </p>
<p> 6. Underlined (u) This is a <u>beautiful </u> world.</p>
<p> 7. Mark (mark) This is a <mark>beautiful </mark> world. </p>
<p> 8. Big (big) This is a <big>beautiful </big> world.</p>
<p> 9. Small (small) This is a <small>beautiful </small> world. </p>
<p> 10. Subscript (sub) This is a <sub>beautiful </sub> world. </p>
<p> 11. Superscript (sup) This is a <sup>beautiful </sup> world.</p>

</body>
</html>
```

h1 - This is a beautiful world.

h2 - This is a beautiful world.

h3 - This is a beautiful world.

h4 - This is a beautiful world.

h5 - This is a beautiful world.

h6 - This is a beautiful world.

2. Emphasis (em) - This is a *beautiful* world.

3. Italics ( ) - This is a *beautiful* world.

4. Strong (strong) This is a **beautiful** world.

5. Bold (bold) This is a beautiful world.

6. Underlined (u) This is a <u>beautiful</u> world.

7. Mark (mark) This is a beautiful world.

8. Big (big) This is a beautiful world.

9. Small (small) This is a beautiful world.

10. Subscript (sub) This is a $_{beautiful}$ world.

11. Superscript (sup) This is a ^{beautiful} world.

Code

```
<!DOCTYPE html>
<html>
<head>
<title>Text Formatting</title>
</head>
<body>

<pre>
Pre (pre)
This is a
      Beautiful World.
</pre>

<p> Delete-Insert (del, ins) This is a <del> beatiful </del> <ins>beautiful </ins> world. </p>
</body>
</html>
```

In Browser, it is displayed as-

```
Pre (pre)
This is a
      Beautiful World.
```

Delete-Insert (del, ins) This is a ~~beatiful~~ beautiful world.

1.5.2 Lists

Lists are used for representing items in a bulleted form and numbered form on a web page. There are three ways in which lists can be presented in a web page - unordered list, ordered list, definition list.

- **Unordered List**
    - <ul> </ul> To create a list with no sequence.
    - <li> </li> encloses the items to be displayed in bulleted form.
- **Ordered List**
    - <ol> and </ol> To create a list with sequence.
    - <li> </li> encloses the items to be displayed as numbered list.
- **Definition lists**
    - <dl> and </dl> To create a list of terminologies with definitions.
    - <dt> </dt> encloses the definition term
    - <dd> </dd> encloses the definition.

11

Code

```html
<!DOCTYPE html>
<html>
<head>
<title>Global Warming</title>
</head>
<body>
<p>
<b>Global warming</b> is the hottest topic of discussion among the people.
<br>Few things done by each of us can surely make a huge difference.

<ul> <b> At community level:</b>
<li>     Shut down computers when not using it. It could reduce CO<sub>2</sub> emission by
83%.
<li>     Always run the dishwasher and washing machine with full load.
<li>     When feeling cold in an air conditioned room, turn the thermostat up by a degree or two.
<li>     Wherever possible go walking.
<li>     Get rooms painted with light beautiful colors. It keeps the house cool.
<li>     Get energy audit done to find ways to reduce energy consumption.
</ul></p>

<ol> <b> Our Nature </b>
<li> Save our earth, save our beautiful nature.
<li> The soothing winds in the woods, the lovely sky,
<li> And beautiful mountains, lakes and ponds and ocean,
<li> These all are the part of this extraordinary
<li> Beautiful and calm nature
<li> Nature which teaches us to be calm, just like winds
<li> Beautiful just like oceans, mountains and lakes
<li> Nature is the most beautiful thing lord has created,
<li> But why is this nature degrading?
<li> Million tons of CO<sub>2</sub> and methane, destroying calmness of air
<li> The excessive cutting of the woods, disturbing Nature's balance
<li> So to be alive and live your life,
</ul>

<dl>
<dt> <b>Print Layout view </b></dt>
<dd> Helps to see how the document will look when it is printed. </dd><br>
<dt> <b>Full Screen Reading view </b></dt>
<dd> Maximizes space available for reading. Hides ribbon. </dd><br>
<dt> <b>Web Layout view </b></dt>
<dd> Allows seeing how the document will appear in a web browser. </dd> <br>
</dl>
</body></html>
```

Global warming is the hottest topic of discussion among the people. Few things done by each of us can surely make a huge difference.

At community level:

- Shut down computers when not using it. It could reduce CO_2 emission by 83%.
- Always run the dishwasher and washing machine with full load.
- When feeling cold in an air conditioned room, turn the thermostat up by a degree or two.
- Wherever possible go walking.
- Get rooms painted with light beautiful colors. It keeps the house cool.
- Get energy audit done to find ways to reduce energy consumption.

Our Nature

1. Save our earth, save our beautiful nature.
2. The soothing winds in the woods, the lovely sky,
3. And beautiful mountains, lakes and ponds and ocean,
4. These all are the part of this extraordinary
5. Beautiful and calm nature
6. Nature which teaches us to be calm, just like winds
7. Beautiful just like oceans, mountains and lakes
8. Nature is the most beautiful thing lord has created,
9. But why is this nature degrading?
10. Million tons of CO_2 and methane, destroying calmness of air
11. The excessive cutting of the woods, disturbing Nature's balance
12. So to be alive and live your life,

Print Layout view
Helps to see how the document will look when it is printed.

Full Screen Reading view
Maximizes space available for reading. Hides ribbon.

Web Layout view
Allows seeing how the document will appear in a web browser.

1.5.3 Links

Links are used for interlinking web pages of same or different websites, different sections of a web page, or to display email addresses. When creating hyperlink, a path is to be provided.

<a href= ..> </a> Encloses the text to be clicked.

```
<!DOCTYPE html>
<html>
<head>
<title>Using Links</title>
</head>
<body>

<p>Click on - <a href="http://www.google.com">Google</a>, to open search engine.</p>
<p>Click on - <a href="http://www.google.com" target = "_blank">Google in new window </a>, to
open search engine in a new window </p>

</body>
</html>
```

In Browser, it is displayed as-

Click on - Google, to open search engine

Click on - Google in new window, to open search engine in a new window.

1.5.4 Tables

- Tables are made of rows and columns.
- <table> </table> It is used to create table.
- <tr> </tr> It is used to specify rows of the table.
- <th> </th> It is used to specify the headings of the columns of the table.
- <td>, </td> It is used to specify the data in the table.
- A table may have text, numbers, graphics list and much more.

The popular tags used with a table are shown in the Table 2.

Table 2. Some key tags for Table in HTML

Tag	Description
<table> </table>	Encloses a table
<th> </th>	Defines a header cell in a table
<tr> </tr>	Encloses a Table row
<td> </td>	Encloses a cell of Table
<caption> </caption>	Defines a table Title
<colspan>	Specifies cells than span many columns
<rowspan>	Specifies cells than span many rows
<thead>	Group the header content in a table
<tbody>	Groups the body content in a table
<tfoot>	Groups the footer content in a table

Code

```
<!DOCTYPE html>
<html>
<head>
<title>Using Tables</title>
</head>
<body>
<table border=4 cellpadding=15px cellsapcing=15px
            align=center width=50% >
<tr>
        <caption> <b>Capitals of Countries </b></caption>
<thead>
        <th>     S.No.    </th>
        <th>     Country </th>
        <th>     Capital </th> </tr> </thead>
<tr align=center>
        <td>     1.           </td>
        <td>     Australia </td>
        <td>     Canberra   </td></tr>
<tr align=center>
        <td>     2.         </td>
        <td>     Bhutan   </td>
        <td>     Thimpu   </td></tr>
<tr align=center>
        <td>     3.         </td>
        <td>     Nigeria </td>
        <td>     Abuja     </td></tr>
<tfoct align=center>
        <td colspan = 3><b>BYE! </b></td> </tfoot>
</table>
</body>
</html>
```

In Browser, it is displayed as-

Capitals of Countries		
S.No.	Country	Capital
1.	Australia	Canberra
2.	Bhutan	Thimpu
3.	Nigeria	Abuja
BYE!		

1.5.5 Images

- <img> </img> is used for including images.
- The following attributes can be used with the images-
    - **src** - to specify location of the image
    - **height and width** - to specify dimensions of the image.
    - **alt** - to display text alternatively, if the image is not displayed.

Code

```
<!DOCTYPE html>
<html>
<head>
<title> Understanding Links</title>
</head>
<body>
<h4> Hibiscus Flower </h4>

<img src="C:\Users\anita\Pictures\Hibiscus.jpg "
       alt="Sorry! The image cannot be displayed now. Pl. try later." height = 300 width="300"
height="300">
<h6> Courtesy: Ajay   </h6>
</body></html>
```

In Browser, it is displayed as-

17

Hibiscus Flower

Courtesy: Ajay

1.5.6 Color Codes

- Colors are set using "RGB" color codes.
- They are represented as hexadecimal values.
- Of the total six digit, each two digit is for the amount of color, red, green, blue, in sequence.
- The colors are generally used in two ways – (1) use name of color, for example, red, green, yellow; or (2) use hexadecimal values, for example, FF0000, 008000, FFFF00.

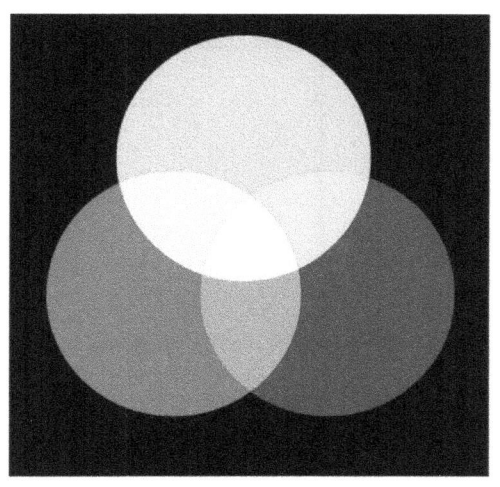

Color Name	RGB Triplet	Hexadecimal	Color Name	RGB Triplet	Hexadecimal
Aqua	(0,255,255)	00FFFF	Navy	(0,0,128)	000080
Black	(0,0,0)	000000	Olive	(128,128,0)	808000
Blue	(0,0,255)	0000FF	Purple	(128,0,128)	800080
Fuchsia	(255,0,255)	FF00FF	Red	(255,0,0)	FF0000
Gray	(128,128,128)	808080	Silver	(192,192,192)	C0C0C0
Green	(0,128,0)	008000	Teal	(0,128,128)	008080
Lime	(0,255,0)	00FF00	White	(255,255,255)	FFFFFF
Maroon	(128,0,0)	800000	Yellow	(255,255,0)	FFFF00

Code

```
<!DOCTYPE html>
<html>
<head>
<title>Using Tables</title>
<style>
thead {color:black;}
tbody {color:blue;}
tfoot {color:red;}
</style>
</head>
<body>
<table border=4 cellpadding=15px cellsapcing=15px bordercolor="brown" bordercolordark=30
            align=center width=50% bgcolor=FFFF00 >
<tr>
        <caption> <b>Capitals of Countries </b></caption>
<thead>
        <th>     S.No.    </th>
        <th>     Country </th>
        <th>     Capital </th> </tr> </thead>
<tr align=center>
        <td>     1.          </td>
        <td>     Australia </td>
        <td>     Canberra  </td></tr>
<tr align=center>
        <td>     2.          </td>
        <td>     Bhutan   </td>
        <td>     Thimpu   </td></tr>
<tr align=center>
        <td>     3.          </td>
        <td>     Nigeria </td>
        <td>     Abuja    </td></tr>
<tfoot align=center>
        <td colspan = 3><b>BYE! </b></td> </tfoot>
</table>
</body>
</html>
```

In Browser, it is displayed as-

Capitals of Countries		
S.No.	Country	Capital
1.	Australia	Canberra
2.	Bhutan	Thimpu
3.	Nigeria	Abuja
BYE!		

1.5.7 Meta data

- Meta data is the data about data.

- The information written in meta data is used by the web browser.

- Meta data is included in between the **<head> </head>** element.

- The code in the head section is *not displayed* in the web browser.

- The meta data includes-

    o Name - to include the author's name

    o Description - to describe the web page/site

    o Keyword - to be used by search engine for indexing

    o Copyright - to include copyright details

Code

```
<!DOCTYPE html>
<html>
<head>
<title>Using meta data</title>
<meta name="Anita" content="My name is Anita">
<meta name="description" content="This is about meta data ">
<meta name="keywords" content="Meta data, Anita, Attributes">
<meta name="copyright" content="It is under Creative Commons">
</head>
<body>
<p> using meta data</p>
</body>
</html>
```

1.6 Tag Summary

Here, Table 3 we present a list of a few tags along with their attributes.

Table 3. Some tags and their attributes

Tags	Attributes	Description
\<Body>	bgcolor	To give background color. default - white
	background	To display image in background of web page
	text	To give text color. default - black
	linkj	Specify color of hyperlink. default - blue
	vlink	Color of link after visited. default - purple
	alink	Color of link when clicked. default - red
	topmargin	Blank area from top edge of page. In pixels (1 inch = 72 pixels)
	leftmargin	Blank area from left edge of page. In pixels (1 inch = 72 pixels)
\<h>	align	Left, right, center
\<p>	align	Alignment of text in paragraph. left, right, ter, justify
\<hr>	size	Thickness of horizontal rule. Default - 3 pixels
	width	Length of horizontal rule. Default - 100%. Value in percentage
	align	Alignment of horizontal rule, left, right and center (default)
	color	Color of horizontal rule. Default - Black color
	noshade	2-D horizontal rule with color. Default - 3D horizontal rule
\<ul>	type	Type of bullets for list items. E.g. \<ul type = square>
\<ol>	type	Type of numbering
	start	Specify start of list sequence number. E.g. \<ol type=A start =2>
\<dl>	compact	Display definition along with the term and not below it
\<img>	src	Address of image
	Height, width	Size of image
	border	Insert a border and specify the thickness
	align	Alignment of image - left, right, top, middle
	alt	When mouse pointer on image, alt text is displayed, like tool tip
\<table>	align	Alignment of table - left(default), right, center

22

	cellspacing	Amount of space between cells. default - 1
	cellpadding	Amount of space between cell border and cell content. default - 2
	bgcolor	To give background color.
	border	Insert a border around the table
	Height, width	Size of table
\<tr\>	align	Alignment of text in row - left(default), right, center
	valign	Alignment of text in row - middle(default), top, bottom
	bgcolor	To give background color for row.
\<td\>	align	Horizontal alignment of cell contents - left(default), right, center
	valign	Vertical alignment of cell contents - middle(default), top, bottom
	bgcolor	To give background color of table row (single cell).
	colspan	Span or merge more than one cell column-wise
	rowspan	Span Span or merge more than one cell row-wise
\<th\>	align	Horizontal alignment of cell heading - left(default), right, center
	valign	Vertical alignment of cell heading - middle(default), top, bottom
	bgcolor	To give background color.
	nowrap	Specifies that line within a cell cannot be broken
	colspan	Span or merge more than one cell column-wise
	rowspan	Span Span or merge more than one cell row-wise

1.7 Summary

➢ *HyperText Markup Language (HTML)* is a language which is used for creating web pages. It is a web authoring software language specifically created for making World Wide Web pages.

➢ *HTML file* is stored with the extension .html or .htm.

➢ HTML consists of *elements* that are the building blocks of a website.

➢ HTML *document* is mainly divided into two parts - Head and Body.

➢ *Head* is the header section of a document. It contains information about a web page.

➢ *Body* element contains body content and is displayed in the web browser.

➢ *Text content* of a web page can be formatted to make it more attractive by using HTML elements such as Headings, Bold, Italics, etc.

➢ *Lists* are used for representing items in a bulleted form, numbered form etc. on a web page.

> *Links* are used for interlinking web pages of same or different websites, different sections of a web page, to display email addresses etc.

> *Tables* are made of rows and columns.

> *Colors* are set using "RGB" color codes.

> *Meta data* is the data about data. It provides information that is used by the web browser.

Task 1: Use HTML to make bio-data

Create your home page using HTML consisting of your photo, name, address and education details as a table and your skill set as a list.

A sample bio-data is as follows-

```
<html>
<head>
<title>My Biodata</title>
</head>
<body>
<table border="02" width=80%>          ← Create outer border of biodata
<tr> <td>
<h1><u>BIODATA </u></h1>

<table style="width:70%">                 ← Write Name info and insert photo
        <tr><td><h3>My Name </h3></td> <td rowspan="4"><img src="C:\Users\anita\Pictures\Boy.jpg"
                                    height = 200 width="200" align=right> </td></td>
        <tr><td><h3> Female, India, 20years </h3></td></tr>
        <tr><td><h3>Contact: 00001111 </h3></td></tr>
        <tr><td><h3>E-mail:ab@gmail.com</h3></td></tr>
</table>

<h2 style="background-color:silver"><u><i><b> Educational qualification </i></u></b></h2>     ← Create silver band with heading     ← Table for educational qualification

<h2><table border="01" width=9% cellspacing="5px" cellpadding="10px" bgcolor = aqua>
<tr><th>Year</th> <th>Degree</th> <th>School/College</th> <th>Subject/Specialization</th> </tr>
<tr align="center"><td>2013</td><td> Graduation </td><td> ABC College </td><td> Data Science</td></tr>
<tr align="center"><td>2011</td><td> XII </td><td> ABC School </td><td>Science</td></tr>
<tr align="center"><td>2009</td><td> X </td><td>ABC School<td> English, Hindi,Maths,Science, Sanskrit</td></tr>
</table></h2>

<h2 style="background-color:silver"><u><i><b>Technical knowledge</i></u></b></h2>
<h2><b><u> Languages known: </u></b></h2>
<ul><li><b> C++ </li><li>Assembly language</li><li>HTML</li></ul>     ← Create List items

<h2 style="background-color:silver"><u><i><b>Personal Information</i></u></b></h2>

<h3><table width=70%>
<tr><td><b>Father's Name:</b> td>   <td>Mr. XYZ</td> </tr> <tr><td><b>Date Of Birth:</b></td> <td>My dob</td></tr>
<tr><td><b>Address:</b></td> <td> My address</td></tr>
<tr><td><b>Languages:</b></td> <td> Hindi and English</td></tr>   </table></h3>     ← Table for Personal Information

<h2 style="background-color:silver"><u><i><b>Declaration</i></u></b></h2>

<p style="font-size:20";> The above information is true to best of my knowledge.<br><br>Yours Truly<br> My name
</td></tr>
</table>          ← Outer border of bio-data closes here
</body>
</html>
```

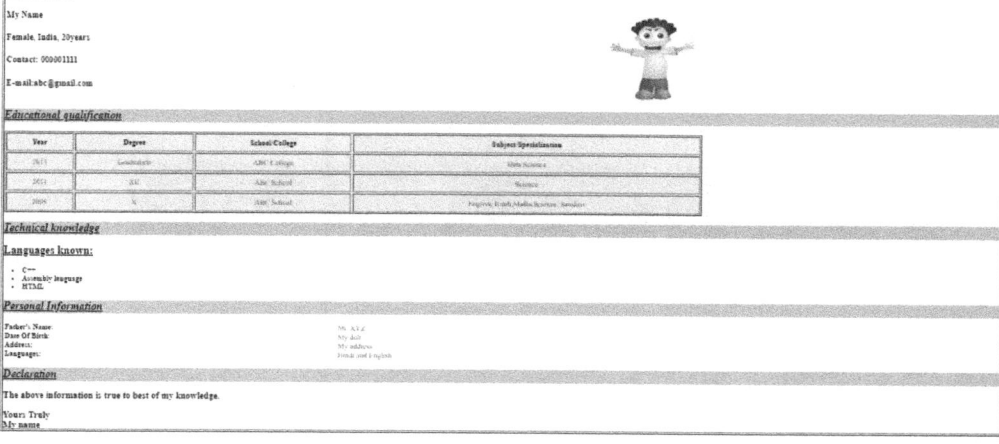

Task 2: Use HTML to make Website

Create the first page of the website as shown in the code below. Then create each page.

```
<html>

<head>
<title>My first webpage</title>
</head>

<body bgcolor="#f5f5f5">

<table width=70% bgcolor="#a80000" align="center">
<tr align="center"><td><br> <h1>My First Website</h1></td></tr>
</table>

<table width=70% align="center" bgcolor="lightpink">
<tr align="center">
<td><b><a style="color: black;" href="home.html">Home</a></b></td>
<td><b><a style="color: black;" href="profile.html">Profile</a></b></td>
<td><b><a style="color: black;" href="research.html">Research</a></b></td>
<td><b><a style="color: black;" href="contact.html">Contact</a></b></td>
<td><b><a style="color: black;" href="others.html">Other Activities</a></b></td>
</table>

</body>
</html>
```

Hyperlinking is been done on each tab.

Test Yourself

Q1	HTML provides ___ levels of heading.
A	Six
Q2	Which tag is used for displaying text with the largest heading size?
A	<h1>
Q3	Which tag is used to make a text visually bold?
A	<b>
Q4	Which tag is used to make a text to be visually displayed in Italics?
A	<i>
Q5	Which tag is used to make a text underlined?
A	<u>
Q6	Which tag is used for indicating paragraphs?
A	<p>
Q7	Which tag is used to create subscripted text?
A	<sub>
Q8	Which tag is used for aligning text to center of a document?
A	< align=center>

Q9	Which tag is used for indicating an unordered list?
A	\<ul\>
Q10	Which tag is used for indicating an ordered list?
A	\<ol\>
Q11	Which tag is used for indicating a definition list?
A	\<dl\>
Q12	Which tag is used for creating hyperlinks
A	\<a href\>
Q13	Which meta name is used for providing author's name?
A	\<meta name="author"\>
Q14	Which meta name is used for providing detailed information about a web page?
A	\<meta name = "description"\>